The Ultimate Key to Successful Blogging

How to Make a Living Blogging about What You Love

By Al W Moe

Introduction

Can you Blog for Profit?

There is no need to turn this book into a college course on Internet infrastructure. You probably aren't interested in the little data bits that course through the veins of cables, modems, and computers to bring you Internet surfing.

What you probably *are* interested in is how to stay at home, away from the usual 9-5 job, and make a good living by just writing your thoughts and experiences on your own blogs. You can do it if you put in the work!

Am I qualified to write this book? Well, I've been writing for the web for ten years now. My first blogs were exceptionally popular websites for two book publishers, Angel Fire Press and Puget Sound Books.

Unfortunately, those sites were sold and eventually dismantled. Not to worry. I've since taken to quite a bit of book and blog ghostwriting, and I maintain several blogs:

Nevada Casino History
(http://www.nevadacasinohistory.blogspot.com)

Author Book Marketing
(http://www.Authorbookmarketing.blogspot.com)

Kindle Book Review Spot
(http://kindlebookreviewspot.blogspot.com)

I'm a book author, but I also love casino gambling. I'm lucky enough to have a casino gambling blog at About.com, part of the New York Times group. I love to write, and blogging informs my readers about what's happening and brings them some entertainment. Ultimately I sell some books, too. Win-win.

Blog is short for weblog, and the entire concept has taken on a life of its own. Writers no longer need to be frustrated by their inability to get their thoughts and ideas into print – now they can fill up page after page with their insights and have those very words carried all over the world via the technology of their computer and the world wide web.

Of course, there is still one catch. Just because the words are out there, does not mean anybody will see them, and what good is publishing your work to the Internet if nobody ever sees it?

This book delves into what blogging is all about, how fun and exciting it can be, and how you can drive thousands of viewers to your blog. Already, a million wordy writers have found they can make excellent money by simply putting their words into Internet Land and capturing the interest and imagination of others. Perhaps you can too.

A blog, or blog site, is much like a website. You can arrange to sell advertising, text links, banner ads, special reports, password-protected access to subscriber-only archives, and your own blog marketing products.

Want to attract thousands of readers, build a solid, quality reputation, and then have your email do your business for you? It's all possible if you follow the information in this book. All you need to do is read a little here, write a lot on your blog, and plan for your future!

Table of Contents

Chapter One

What is a Blog?

Blog is a shortened name for Weblog. Over the past few years, writers have found that they can have an impact on all types of events around the world by simply posting their thoughts in their blogs. A blog is a personalized Web journal that provides an interactive forum for you and your readers.

You post your thoughts, views, rants and raves about your life, your own world order, and anything else that comes to mind. Your readers offer their opinion about your musings, and you proceed to write new entries called posts, updates, or just blogs, on whatever schedule you prefer.

Blog sites allow you the "owner" or "editor," to add artwork, music, polls, and just about anything else you can think of to keep your readers interested. Of course, the most important element is your continued input, which needs to be honest, informative and interesting. Humor goes a long way, but many blogs are of a political or business nature and are doing exceedingly well, even without the fun and humor I prefer when I'm reading and writing. But now, I'm getting ahead of myself.

A true blog is simply a journal or newsletter that is updated on a regular basis. It is intended for readers of all types, and you, the blogger, manage both the input and the readership. Your input is your "brand," and you manage your readership with input – readers interested in what you have to say will come back often, those who don't, won't. Pretty simple.

Blogs provide a personalized feel and give readers a chance to leave comments, unlike most traditional news outlets.

If you have a love for pottery, you can post your successes and failures with the latest pottery wheel, different clay types, and the kiln you use. Or, if you love the Dallas Cowboys, you can let your readers know how you feel about the last game or the last play that busted them out of the playoffs.

Blogs can be password protected so only your own group of friends can join in reading and discussions, or you can open your heart and mind to the whole world. The wonder world of the Amazon Kindle can also help you attract readers, and capture those who are willing to pay a small fee to blog along.

If you haven't taken a look at any blog hosts, run to your computer and try a few links like *Blogdrive.com*; *Blogomaster.com*; *Blogsavy.com*, *Blogetery.com* – or just type *blog host* into your search engine and then click on links until you have an idea of what is available. Most are free.

CNN, ESPN, and plenty of other news sites are now offering news stories and features that ask for opinions from readers. These are popular because the top responses are posted for everyone to see. Let's face it; people like to see their name in print, even if it's just their email address of just a last name with the few comments they left.

So, today's news is not solely featured on traditional newspaper websites. Blogs have entered the fray. The difference is that newspapers still consider themselves to be the "be all, end all" of quality news. The writers and editors still do the same job as ten years ago, while a blogger presents their own view, much like a newspaper columnist does – without the traditional handcuffs placed on them by their editors or the corporate advertising that pays for newspapers to be published.

Because blogging has become mainstream, many newspaper columnists are now offering their own blogs – a natural, but sometimes frustrating development.

The Internet now boasts over 30 million individual blogs, and more are coming every day. Many blog readers provide support simply by reading the daily offering at their favorite sites. Advertising rates for Internet websites are most often set by viewership – the more "hits" on a website, the higher the cost for advertising. Constant readers also provide income through link usage, donations, and the purchase of "swag" and blog-related paraphernalia.

Swag stands for the "stuff we all get," and is often related to what everybody that joins a local golf tournament might get as tee prizes, or what every attendee at the *Oscars* might receive. But savvy bloggers are selling shirts, coffee cups – Frisbees; just about anything you can think of that they can put their name on. And, it seems to be working.

Advertising merchandise marketing is still a strategic device for keeping the "buzz" going for all types of business ventures. Your blog can, and in my humble, although sometimes warped opinion, should be a viable business. I love to write. For more than twenty years I've added my two cents to magazines, trade papers, websites, and all manner of educational and informative sources, but I still like to be paid.

Ever driven a Jaguar? It doesn't suck. You may not get a chance to prove that to yourself, however, if you don't get paid for your writing.

Chapter Two

You are Your Blog

The most important aspect of a successful blog is the content you provide for your readership. Whether you are providing all of the writing, or are making your blog into a type of portal, when people with similar interests come to see what's happening before leaving your site via one of your links, you must have interesting content. But what comes next? What makes you successful?

Only you can decide what you consider success, but if you want to make money, you need to think of your blog as a business, and yes, your time invested *must* be counted as both an asset, and expense. Without your writing, you have very little to offer, but if you spend countless hours doing the writing and nobody visits, well, I'd prefer to be at the park with my six-year-old than spending all my time at the computer. And you?

You can make a solid income by first attracting visitors to your site, and then selling your services. Your blog can sell the promotional items mentioned earlier, but you will make or break on the income you produce from advertising sales and link income. Links on your sites that connect to other sites, whether another blogger, a business like Amazon, or through click-bank sales via Yahoo! or Google Adwords will provide you with some income. The more "hits" your site gets, the more customers you can send to your advertisers.

Check out dozens of blog spots each day, and you will see what is working for the highest rated sites. Feel free to use their success as your base for starting, and comparing your blog. Don't expect to be able to do everything they do, right off the bat, but strive to go in the direction they are pointing.

Your blog, again, if you want to make a profit, has to have a solid financial foundation. That does not mean you need a lot of money to get started; it means you need to follow a financial plan that takes advantage of what you have to offer, and what you need to supply. You aren't really selling what you started your blog for, now are you?

No. You started your blog to deliver your word to the world. Without you, the blog doesn't exist. You need to provide input, and your readership will do the rest – without thinking about it, without feeling pressured, without a care, because you supply what they need – YOU.

You are the supplier, just like your local produce supplier provides fresh fruits and vegetables to the markets in your area; you provide fresh ideas and thoughts. And, like the businesses that your produce supplier visits each day, you visit homes, libraries, and businesses too. You do it by having your readers' click onto your blog or website to get their daily fill of the news and events in the world – or just in your world.

While you supply your readers with tidbits of your world, you will be supplying your advertisers with a ready audience of potential buyers! The traffic you produce (which many blogs now count in the millions per month) is the lifeblood of your site. The more eyes on your blog, the more eyes on the advertising – and your advertisers pay you based on those eyes, and on "hits."

So, you are selling yourself at all times. You sell your wit and wisdom, your expertise, your overall fun and knowledge about many subjects, even if the most important subject is *your life.*

There are successful newspaper columnists all over the world who do no more than providing a daily offering of events in their life. They talk about sports, their families, their cars, the price of gas, food, entertainment, you name it, and they get paid for it. You will be doing the same. The better you are at entertaining, the more you can make as a blog writer.

Miami Herald humor columnist Dave Barry comes to mind when I think of a columnist who talks specifically about his life. He rarely mentions any earth-shattering ideas, but his columns have led to a very successful career as a book author. He writes about daily events, even if it is nothing more than his dog chasing a squirrel. I don't expect anybody is reading this book to produce the humor Barry does on such a regular basis, but you can drive thousands of people to your site every day if you provide entertainment. It really is that simple.

The text links, banner ads, and click-trough's that your site also offers your readers will be the basis for your income, but as mentioned earlier, the sale of merchandise also provides income and keeps the name of your blog in circulation. A relationship (read: good relationship!) with other bloggers and website owners can also produce thousands of referral link viewers for your blog. Get along – get paid more!

Chapter Three

Your Own Blog Content

Now that you have an idea of how a blog operates let's look at how easy it really can be to create your site. Most blog sites automate the publishing process, so you are not required to write any code, or worry about installing anything. Go ahead, be a Techno-goof like me, and you can still put together a great looking site!

Technological advances over the past few years provide a very simple basis for customers to set up websites and blog pages. There is no need to understand HTML or any programming language to produce very professional-looking sites in a fraction of the time programmers used to spend on even the most rudimentary web jobs.

Don't let a fear of the unknown keep you from your goals. Fear is all in your mind (unless you have to eat Brussels sprouts, then the fear is in your mouth), so don't be a wimp. The process is so simple, even a young child or presidential candidate can make a website these days – so long as they follow the directions provided by the hosting service.

If you have a web browser (such as Internet Explorer or Firefox) and an Internet connection, you are ready to get started. Having an IP (Internet Provider) that does not rely on dial-up is also important. You can still use a dial-up provider, but you will find at times that the slower service is not conducive to your desire to "get the word out."

Designing your site should involve your best sense of what you want to provide to your readers, and customer service is obviously an important element. The better your readers can get around your site, the more likely they are to enjoy their stay and return for subsequent visits. However, the main thing that differentiates your site from those of other bloggers is you.

Your site truly needs to reflect your tastes. You can't design everything according to what you *think* your readers want to see. You need to customize things to fit your tastes. Certainly, this means not everybody will be happy with your offerings, but you need to develop a core of happy surfers who return because they like the *real you* if you will allow me to be so direct.

There is no way to produce a daily script of writing that takes every person into account. Make yourself happy, and do your best to actively support the readers who like your particular style and panache!

Now that I have made the simple point that you need to reflect yourself, you also need to walk that tight-wire between courageous individuality and banal, obsessive self-indulgence. You do need to consider your average reader, and you do need to provide value for their time.

And what, exactly will you be posting about besides yourself? This isn't a high school essay contest, but you do need to have some theme for your blog. If it is just your view, that's all right, but there might be a chance you want to narrow that down a bit.

If you go to one of the most popular blog search engines, *Technorati.com*, you will find several groups of similar blog types: sports, recreation, politics, business, etc. This helps reader's find sites of interest, and you will want to ally yourself with some kind of group – if for no other reason than to make it easy for new visitors to find you. Search around, and you will find blogs that feature everything you can imagine. You don't need to "fit in," but you do need to "fit" somewhere.

Technorati lists the top 100 blogs (under the tab "Blogger Central"), and popular blogs get thousands of page views each day, and specific topics (from as few as one, or as many as 100 or more blogs) can generate as many as 100,000 responses. The traffic that flows through the most popular blogs is phenomenal.

Content is king, so you need to provide relevant, exciting content to be the ruler of a successful blog domain. You can still have a lot of fun with a blog, even if you are just providing input for family and friends, but to be successful financially, you need to work hard to get your traffic up to numbers that will also attract advertisers.

Once all the bricks are in place, your blog can run itself with only some daily input and words of wisdom from you. Now isn't that where you would like to be headed?

Chapter Four

If you want to be on top of your game, every day, you will need to scan the Internet each day for the latest news. Of course, as you do this, you are getting the news *after* many others have. This is still the quickest way to find information, but you have to realize that others are on top of their game also.

They are doing just what you are and writing their opinions about what they are researching too. To be successful, you need to provide specific insight or at least an entertaining edge to your reporting of the trends of the day.

You don't have to work alone as a blogger. Some blogs are a combination of many contributors. Some are multi-contributor freeform blogs, and some are more structured. If you want to work as part of a team, you can join a group and cultivate a following of your own.

Doing so allows you a chance to be part of an established group, but will more than likely reduce your ability to provide a completely unedited version of your words. You will also be without the benefit of income from your advertising deals.

You will, however, have the advantage of a ready audience, and there is no reason that your writing can't point to another blog site (your own) where you *are* in complete control.

While you ruminate about your likes and dislikes and think about whether you should try blogging on your own, or as part of a group, you might want to think about who you are.

You should be at a point now where you are seriously thinking about doing that daily writing – and you probably can't wait to get started, but give it a little while longer before you jump in.

Ask yourself now – what do I want to accomplish by offering my views to the world. Are you going to write about a hobby (coin collecting, taxidermy, model airplane building, bowling, cat painting) or about your favorite sport (kayaking, skiing, in-home car keys finding) or about politics, college courses, business to business website management, or what?

So, pull out some paper and a pencil, pen, or crayon, and write down some answers to the question of what you want to accomplish, and what answers you want to receive from your readers. Yes, you will get responses at your blog, and you should be prepared to accept some criticism, and with hope plenty of accolades for being so brave and honest in your writing. Don't be a bloggie baby! Tell the truth in your writing.

Now, do you also realize that your blog can provide a lot of great information *for* you? Ask questions and get answers from your guests. Believe me; readers love to provide information. However, just so you don't ever get stuck for things to write about, take that crayon we talked about earlier and put down a few things about yourself.

Where were you born and what state do you live in is a good start. You don't want to give every detail about yourself to your readers, but you do want to share some background information. You might get into your upbringing, your lifestyle, your cultural background – and even what languages you speak. Was your father a butcher, baker, or did he drive you to school in the company hearse?

Do you love the city, or like to hear a *moo*? Do you ride a bike, like to walk, drive a Ferrari, or travel about on your pogo stick? It matters to you, and it will matter to your readers.

Are you happy with your lot in life, or are there things you would like to change? Is it even possible to change those things you are thinking about? Could they be changed if enough people wanted the same thing? Can you band together with your readers? Are we leading towards a political discussion? Perhaps, but that might be good. If you don't wish to, don't go there. Just take out your machete and make your own path. You do own a machete, right? If you don't, how will you cut down some of the over-worded babble you were thinking of putting into your first blog?

Are you an expert in any fields? Are you out in left field? Do you make dolls fitted with dresses you sew from old clothes, or do you design nuclear power plants? What's the scoop – there's a story waiting to be told, and now you are the one to tell it.

Why did you get Internet service? Do you have a good provider, or does your service suck? Do you use email exclusively, or do you still use snail mail or carrier pigeon? Where do you go on the web? Do you hit that email first, or do you go to the sites that feature the restoration of Mayan ruins? What's the scoop?

As you get readers to your blog, what kind of an experience do you want them to have? Do you just want them to have a pleasant time, or do you want them to be challenged? Should they get mad, upset, even infuriated by your writing, or will you only provide daily sunshine? Let's face it, controversy sells. So does humor. Insight and good writing sells too, but not always as much.

Although readers might not be paying a penny to read your views, what *would* they pay to read about? What area of expertise do you possess that they might be interested in? What would you pay to read on a daily, weekly, or monthly basis? Can you provide something that a casual reader might find fascinating enough to pay for? You probably can, and that might be an area that you want to touch on – regularly.

Don't be afraid that you won't have anything to offer your readers. I guarantee you that there are many things about yourself, your life, and your beliefs that will attract readers. You are unique. In many ways, you are unlike any other person in the world. However, you will still have plenty in common with millions of people surfing the web and just looking for something interesting to pass the time with!

Have you thought any more about a theme yet? There it is again, another old high school bug-a-boo. It won't hurt, honest. Just think about a few things that you are interested in writing about. Now cruise over to your computer and type in the things you are interested in, one at a time, and do a quick search. This should expand your thinking for each subject.

Now you probably have a different problem: How to narrow down your ideas! Well don't worry, you are just getting started. There is plenty of time to make your decisions, and you may find that after starting your blog on a certain topic that you don't enjoy writing about it. So, fuggedabodit.

You also might be worried about what you name your blog. Certainly, there are problems with some names, but who would have thought that eBay would be an Internet auction site? Your content will dictate your success, not your name.

If you want to take a stab at a few names, type an idea into your web browser and see what it links to. What ideas come up?

You can do the same with the thesaurus on your word processor, or on the Internet. You might even punch in the name at a domain selling site and see what comes up. When the name you want is not available, they often give similar names as a second choice – you never know where that idea is going to come from.

Whether or not your brand is relevant to your content, it will quickly develop one relevant attribute: a reputation. Everyone who reads your blog will come away with an impression, either good or bad. They will like it or they won't. Surprisingly, that's not the most important issue for your blog, because not even your most loyal reader is going to like or agree with what you have to say every day.

The important issue is whether that reader believes your blog is important. If it's not important, said reader probably wouldn't return even if they enjoyed some aspects of your writing – because there are just too many other blogs out there in Web Land.

If a reader finds your blog insightful, entertaining, and relevant, they will return whether they agree or disagree with your commentary or your layout. Be serious about your content, your offerings, and your readers – and they will become serious readers of your daily input.

Technology blogs need to be accurate. Don't offer insight to technology that is dated, or just plain wrong. You can't offer political commentary from last month's candidate debate. You need to write about last night's debate, or the one coming up tomorrow! Stay current.

If you design a blog about fire eating, what type of combustible materials you use is relevant, but what color tricycle you rode to work last night probably isn't. The farther out you go from your original subject, the more dangerous the waters. If you go out into choppy waters, your readers – those rowing your boat – will probably abandon you. If this happens, you eventually capsize and drown.

Blog readers base their views on what they read. If your reputation is well established, they will read, and quote you. Your reputation is everything, so tend that garden well. Build your site, your words, and your reputation carefully, and don't blow it all by taking your frustrations out on your readers during a bad-hair, or brain, morning. Know your subject, present your case well, and move on.

Chapter Five

Design

Tried and true may be safe, but there is no reason to accept what is offered as the best course. When creating the design for your blog, you *should* look at many blog sites, and you *should* see which ones are popular, easily navigated, and enjoyable, but you don't need to copy everything they have. And what do they have?

What's available at a low cost, you might be asking. You can go to Blogger and be part of the Google network and you'll have a website set up in minutes. There are changeable themes, ways for your to monetize your pages, and built-in designs. Or, you can be a little more creative and go to Wordpress and start there. It's free for a standard blog, and you can always update – and add your own domain name for a small fee. Take a look at both, but keep in mind there are hundreds of blog builders.

It's a good idea to emulate the successful model that a quality blog provides, but you need to strive to exceed what is out there. You are ultimately in charge of everything on your blog. Take advantage of your predecessors by seeing what they use to provide a quality site – but make your own brand!

You might want to take some time right now and look at more blogs. Consider going back to *Technorati* and looking at the top 100 blogs. What do you see? Blogs that have risen to the top based on content, readership, and of course, traffic. Top blogs also are counted by things like the number of other blogs that link back to them.

When you find blogs you personally enjoy, take note of their page layout. What is it that you like – color, type style, font, openness, clutter, what is it? Put your crayon to use again. Write down what you like, and what you don't. What ideas do you now have?

What do the best sites offer to readers in the way of links to previous entries, or to reader responses? What works best or is easiest for you to navigate around. Steal ideas from every decent site and make your own super site! Go ahead; it's perfectly all right to copy the masters. Take the best from all over and make it your own!

Now, let's take a look at branding. Ever heard of Coca-Cola? Now, what image comes to mind? You probably think of the style of the letters on a bottle of Coke, or the red color of the packaging. Well, you aren't alone. Whether things go better with Coke or not, there is virtually nobody in the world, who is using a computer, who does not have a clear image of coke and their trademark, their bottle, or the taste of the soft drink itself.

Is it all just clever marketing? Perhaps. But except maybe the use of a polar bear in some ads, Coke has presented a specific image – and we all know the brand. Choose wisely, grasshopper, and when you get things perfect, don't introduce *New Coke*, all right?

Let's say your idea is to talk about chili, your favorite food. You might use subtle colors of green and red – you can stray to artwork that includes campfires or even a firehouse, if you offer a really hot (yes, that should be spicy) recipe. However, a beach scene probably doesn't fit too well. Make your readers "see" your blog, even when they only read the name again. If you can do this, then through the subtle (and sometimes not so subtle) use of marketing and branding, your readers will remember your blog when they see objects in their daily life. When this happens, you've got 'em.

Of course, this only happens when you also give them stunning images in your writing. The writing still comes first, but don't get caught up using crap for your blog site. Don't use cheesy clip art that looks like it was made in the 1950's unless you happen to blog about what grandma and grandpa call the "good old days."

Engadget.com is the web world's answer to *Consumer Reports*. The end of their masthead that shows their name, *amplifies* it, with a tiny drawing of sound waves coming off the final "t" in their name. Simple, but still effective. They've gone to a subtle style of design, but each news item has a photo. And what do they ask the readers to do? Answer questions, such as "What would you change on your cell phone?"

This provides them with input, gets readers engaged, and creates interest. And where do some ads point? To *Weblogs, Inc.* (*weblogsinc.com*) where you can create your blog, get paid to blog, read blogs without editing, and do your marketing.

The Cable and *Ars Technica* round out the top three blogs at *Technorati*. *Ars Technica* has adopted a fairly simple design and looks more like a traditional website. *The Cable* looks more like a blog to me, and they make sure you know you can get your fill each day with their email service, *without* the bells and whistles of amazing background and design. Content is number one!

As for the font to use for your writing, simple is best. Times New Roman has been a favorite for years, it is simple, easy on the eyes, and people are used to it. Don't use Wingdings or some crazy font that distracts from the message you are trying to get across. The blog site you choose will have a default font – it's the default because it is the most popular, and probably there is a reason for that to be the case.

Most blogs have a backup system for generating income: ads, or links. Some sites offer only advertising, keeping readers from leaving home unless they might buy something. Others are more than happy to allow their readers to jump ship and head to another blog or any number of other sites via a link. Have your links open in a new web page, and you'll still have them on your site too!

A link can be something simple like a text-link that when clicked on, will take a reader to another website. Links do your readers a favor, because you have given them a chance to keep surfing. And, you get the bonus of having a chance to earn income.

Everything on your page needs to contribute to your page, and your links are no exception. Organize them in a manner that your readers can navigate easily, such as alphabetically, or by subject. They should also contribute to your blog's content. If your blog is about candy manufacturing, you can link to different candy manufacturers'. You don't want to link to the local pizza joint.

Most blog and website software come complete with different templates, and each can be designed with a sense of style and manageability. Choose one that fits your own style – and enhance it the best you can. Take advantage of the features that are already built-in, like an archive, reader response, email subscriptions, but add enough of yourself to stand out in your reader's minds.

Now, drop your jump rope and skip around the web playground to check out a few of the web hosts again and see what their packages offer. You probably already know what you like and would use on your site. Can you insert objects like a counter, so readers know how many others have landed on your web planet? Can you put in current news, weather, or other objects (in tech lingo, an object is a tiny bit of code) you want on your site to make it unique to provide useful content for your readers? Everything you add to your blog needs to have a purpose. Don't overload your readers.

If we get back to that "theme" idea, you should be focusing on a group of things that create a single message with a unique harmony. Don't clutter things up. You want everyone who visits your site to consider returning. The number one rule of the blogging business is to create repeat business. You want repeat visitors – the traffic is cash for a blogger as it is for most any website.

And how do you get repeat visitors? Well, aside from the "first impression" of your design and layout, up to date information is vital. And, it has to be entertaining. Build your blog just as a bricklayer builds a wall: from the bottom up.

Feel free to make your first entry a kind of introduction if you wish, but I'd be more inclined to have a link at the top or bottom of my site with an "about us," or similar name that leads to a more detailed picture of who you are. Better make this a good read – that's where some visitors start.

So, let's say that's the bottom of your wall – an introduction, now you need to keep the mortar warm and add new bricks *every single day*. When you start, you might be adding more than one brick a day – and that's fine too. But don't do so much writing that your content becomes dull. When I read dull, I click away quick.

Keep in mind that your weblog is a published piece of writing from your own mind. Write what you like, what you know, and be informative. Write with carefree abandon if you want, but don't steer away from the truth. Just make sure you keep it relative and consistent, always be accurate, and try to be as timely as possible. You build your reputation with every new brick you place on that wall. Keep writing even when you don't want to. Put something new there for your readers. After all, you started building, and they want to see progress. You don't have to build the Great Wall of China, but you better be headed somewhere.

One of my favorite blogs was started in a tiny town in Washington State. They reviewed restaurants and provided information about the owners, their bill of fare, prices, and it was great. However, they ran out of restaurants. So, guess what they did?

No, they didn't move on to another city, they stopped publishing. Now I haven't visited for a while, and I won't pass on their site – because they lost my interest. I clicked back three times and got nothing. And believe you me; I went back two more times than the usual blog reader will. Don't quit on your readers.

Chapter Six

Consistency

Do you know what a city planner does? They try their best to gauge the future needs of the community. In doing so, they plan for growth. Think of your blog or website as a city. It doesn't matter exactly where the library is, or where the mall is, but the roads better connect to something. Your site navigates like a city, with certain exits reaching certain destinations.

When you take a left on Elm Street, you just *know* it's going to take you to grandma's house, it's always been there. Now how are you going to feel if one day you make that left turn and the grocery store is there instead of grandma's house? Sure, you can still get your cookies, but they won't taste nearly as good.

Don't toss your readers a curveball and make them relearn your layout. Design your site well, and keep it consistent. Some change in your city will have to take place as you grow, but understand that even if you are building a needed hospital, somebody is going to be displaced, and people are going to get redirected and lost.

Change may be good in the long run, but even change for the good is hard for people. Human beings are creatures of habit, and change makes us work harder. That's not what readers of your blog want. They want to forget their daily routine and be entertained for a while. Do not make your precious visitors jump through hoops to get their daily vitamin dose of your prose.

Experiment on some different entry styles (your front page, or index), fonts, colors, and layouts until you find something that you enjoy. Now do some yoga. When you come back, see if you still like what you *thought* was perfect. If it still looks good, that's great. If not, keep experimenting. Mozart may have been able to compose straight to a finished score, but most writers and designers need to experiment. Don't be lazy, and don't be in too big a hurry.

I greatly appreciate a line of blog entries that look similar. I want the headline to be the same text style, the same font size, and the same design – followed by the weblog writing. Consider this a start, and work from there. Consistency is important. If you want to change one log a little because it is so very important (your readership tripled is important, your cat threw up is not), you *may* want to offer a headline in another color. I'll try not to hate it.

If you set your blogs up like bricks in a straight line, each one will be the same size. Since you write a different amount of words on any given day, you solve this problem by having a link from that consistent brick to *the rest of the story*.

"More behind the fold," is a way that many blogs identify their links. Some say simply, "more" or "read more," just like a newspaper says "continued on page xxx." Readers get bored easily. If they can only see one entry on your page, and it doesn't grab them, they will surf away. You need to offer several logs for them to read a sentence or two from.

If you are writing about current events, you need to be aware that the information you grabbed from another website, your newspaper, or a local news show, needs to be quoted. You have to attribute the work that went into the story before you took it.

If it is general knowledge, it is in the public domain. However, if you mention that the exact population of Calcutta on the third day of May 1955 was xxx, then you want to quote your source. And if you have the need to consider more about copyright issues (you do), there are blogs and websites to set you straight.

If you do quote a source, such as an article on a website, it's always nice to include a link to the original story. Readers will appreciate it, the website will appreciate it, and they, in turn, may offer a return favor to you at a point in the future.

By now, most people know they can't share their music files with all of their friends – because it's against the law in most countries. But some people think they can use photos for their website that are also under copyright. You don't have the right to use your favorite Ansel Adams photo of Yosemite as your blog page background. There are, however, many photos, and even written passages and eBooks that are shareware or offered for free reprint.

Another thing to remember is that your blog will be available in many different nations. What do you suppose the name World Wide Web refers to? That's right, and if all goes well for you, you *will* have readers from all over the planet taking a look at your work. Nervous? Don't be. Just make sure you write the truth.

The one defense for the charge of slander and libel is truthfulness. If you express or imply something to be truthful, and it is not, you may be charged with a crime. If your blog states facts only, you have a defense against the charge of libel (a harmful statement in a fixed medium, especially writing).

If you want to offer some images on your site, you may want to offer an expanded view. This can be offered via a hyperlink that opens the image in another browser. Any time you link to something, you probably want that link to open in a new browser page. If you don't, your viewers may not come back to your blog!

Engadget uses several photos, because each one shows the product the blog is featuring. However, the images are different sizes and obviously different colors. I don't personally like the varying sizes and would prefer all images to be the same size. However, who's going to listen to this line of reasoning when *Engadget* is one of the hottest blogs on the planet?

You have a lot of leeway with your images, but I caution you against going wild. If you present a crazy, haphazard page, you will probably only retain crazy, haphazard readers. And while that may be a very large audience, it's still not going to be the audience you want coming to visit you each and every day – sending comments and demanding attention. Honest.

While you are finishing the bricks in your wall, let's return to the city you have designed. If you decide to write about the mayor, it is very helpful to have a photo to go along with your blog. Photos are usually available from the mayor's office, often online. If you decide to tell your readers about the mayor's latest speech, it is very helpful if you have a copy available for them to link to.

The speech is probably available somewhere in the mayor's office, and if it can be hyperlinked, that is helpful. If it is not available, you can make your own link with a hardcopy turned into a PDF file, JPEG or GIF image.

Staying consistent can be an issue for similar blogs. For instance, if you use the same symbol for the mayor's speeches each time, readers can go quickly to that image and read what they are looking for. The image might be something like the state seal, flag, or something that makes more of a statement. If you think everything the mayor talks about is trash, well, you get (or can get) the picture.

If you do link to a photo from another site, get permission or know that the other site will somehow benefit from the link. If not, you are taking something away from the other website – bandwidth.

Bandwidth is a measurable commodity. A network allows only so much free bandwidth before they charge additional fees to the user. When a visitor on your site clicks a link to another site to view a photo, bandwidth is used (more with a photo than with text), and charged against the website. Not yours, but the one hosting the photo.

Don't start off your career as a blogger by being a bandwidth thief. That's not the kind of reputation you want to have. Host your own images, and you have the ability to resize them to your exact needs. Make sure they are of the pixels and size asked for by your host. If you don't, an image will load slowly, and most surfers hate to wait.

Also, if you host your own images, then you know they will be there when somebody links to *your site*. If your blogs are insightful and entertaining, you will get linked to, and you want that image to still be available, not pulled from another site!

You can host your images on your own ISP (Internet Service Provider). Your provider may offer all the server space you need. Make sure you can expand the amount of space in the future to accommodate the growth your new blog will experience.

Do not sign up with a free host that offers a tiny amount of free space but charges large fees for extra space. You don't want to have to move your blog and lose what you have put into it or feel like you are being held hostage by your host and paying ransom to keep your blog available to your readers.

Your archive of past blogs is very valuable. That is content that will be referred to and accessed on a regular basis by both yourself and your readers. Make sure your archive is easily accessible to your visitors.

The main page of your blog displays the work you have done in the past few days – your most recent posts. Each needs to be given a specific name, and later, they can be retrieved. For the posts that are already archived, you need to assure that your readers can find logs either by name or by date.

Those logs will be available on your site, and can still be accessed by search engines. Your words now have a kind of immortality. Don't take this gift for granted. Create crap, and you will be forgotten. Mold your word clay into beautiful pottery and your words will be searched for and read – and repeated – for years to come.

The larger your archive, the more references there are on the Internet to you and your work – your words – your reputation. Blogging might not make you much money to begin with, but you can grow a successful garden if you tend it well.

Chapter Seven

Becoming a Relevant Portal

If you love to write, and want nothing more than to bring a little cheer to a few readers each day, well, that's great. Good for you. The world needs more people like you. But, if you want to make some money, maybe enough to be a writer who can fill the cupboards with the fruit of their labor, you need to generate traffic.

Ten years ago, one of the hottest things for sale were web portals. Designers set them up as shopping portals, or they were sold as "themes" such as baseball, cars, or most anything that is popular.

The idea was that when people entered keywords into a search engine, the portal would come up and surfers would click on the link. Once there, they would find something else of interest and click away, but the owner of the portal would make money from advertising. Is Google a portal? Yes, the most successful in the world.

When your home page is Google (or Yahoo! or MSN, etc.), you are a wonderful customer for that portal. Every day you start there and read ads, click on links that provide income for the portal, and then buy things that may or may not also provide a share of the purchase price to the portal. If you are saying, whoa, how do I get in on this, well, that's what this whole book is about!

Your blog, as much fun as it may be to write, needs to become a relevant portal. People interested in your writing will come back on a regular basis and use your site as a portal for the advertisers that pay you for a presence on your site.

To be relevant, you need to provide quality writing in a timely manner, and if you happen to attract a large audience, advertisers will be happy to pay you well to be represented on your pages. If you think this is wrong, well God bless you but move along; you're bothering me.

As a relevant portal, your readers get accustomed to visiting you regularly for your insight, expertise, humor, etc. Other blogs that link to you will do so with the knowledge that you have valuable content. And as readers return, your traffic numbers rise. Unlike your local freeway, where traffic is to be avoided, web traffic is good. It's the lack of traffic that's a killer.

You can head to *Godaddy.com* and make your own website in a short amount of time. They will host your site on their server, and charge you a monthly fee. It's a simple process these days. However, depending on what you want from a website, or now, a blog host site, you need to ask yourself some questions. I already know the answer, because I want you to make money with your writing. But I'm still going to ask you, just in case you want to be different.

Do you want to choose from three blog designs, or do you want enough choices that you won't look like everybody else? Do you want to host your own ads and make some money? Do you want to have reports available that detail where your readers are coming from, which pages they hit, how long they stayed, etc.?

If you answered yes to any of the above, well, it's a trick question because they weren't yes or no, they were multiple choice! The bottom line is that if you want to be in business (and remember we are not Enron here, we actually want to make a profit), you want options.

You want to make your blog in your image. You are the God of your site – create what you like and be true to it. Write daily, write well, create traffic, and create income.

Blogger.com is owned by Google, as I mentioned before. Yeah, they may be a good start when looking for a host. Go for free, and in five minutes you can set up your blog, use their "drag and drop" elements, upload photos, and start writing. You can accept viewer comments, delete what you don't like, provide free access or limit your readers, and find other blogs like yours to link to. All in less than an hour.

Blog-City.com also offers quick access to an account. They have templates to choose from and require no knowledge of HTML to design a new blog. Basic applications are free. Want more – pay more.

Blogdrive.com is another free blogging host. They offer tagboards, RSS feeds, graphics ready to put into place. Nice and easy.

Blogspot.com is like the above. They have free image hosting, and setting up your blog should take no more than ten or fifteen minutes. If you know HTML, you have the option of designing additional layout features.

Xanga.com also offers limited free services to provide "part time" bloggers a chance to get their feet wet. If the wet feet feel nice, you can add services for standardized fees. And then, consider Wordpress again.

If you have heard of *Wordpress.com*, it's because their blog software is so user-friendly. I use it on several sites and have no issues – but you need to download it and find a host – and a host costs money. So, after looking at these few examples, simply input "blog hosts" in your browser, or "free blog hosting" and see what comes up – too many to name. Search, and ye shall find.

Free blog hosts do not provide you with an easy to find URL (that's the name your site goes by on the web). If you do business, you probably want to make it at least a little easier for a surfer to find you, even if you don't want to pay for your own hosting.

A simple solution is to use a site-forwarding service like *MyDomain.com*. They will sell you a domain name for $9.99, and then charge you to forward your traffic. Better yet, consider starting fresh:

Another solution is to pay a monthly fee for web space and purchase a blog software package with all the attributes you want. You will have to buy a domain name, but that was the whole idea here, and the monthly fee will be a little more than at a regular blog host.

However, you will have a good deal more control over your site, plus all the features the software provides. In the long run, if you can handle loading the software (it's easy, but time-consuming) and doing your own design, it will be better for you. Check out different software packages and see what you think. Yahoo! and Homestead.com have monthly packages that are inexpensive, but harder to be creative with.

Chapter Eight

Playing in Traffic

No, no, it's all right this time. Go ahead and play in traffic. In fact, you need to be thrust in the middle of it to make a living on the Internet. The life of a blog is traffic, the visitors who visit your blog day after day, sometimes even multiple times throughout the day.

Paying for Google Adwords, or Yahoo! advertising or MSN search advertising will get a few readers to your site. But the cost is high. Is it worth it to pay a quarter for every click to your blog? How about fifty-cents or more? You can drive traffic to your site this way, but there are some other ways you might consider first.

Traffic exchanges, like web-click exchanges from ten years ago, are a cheap alternative. Unfortunately, it's s time-consuming. You sign-up to view other bloggers sites, and bloggers come to your site to look around. The time you spend looking at other blogs is matched by other blog owners, looking at your site.

Is this a good use of time? If you like to read blogs, it could be. If you want ideas for your blog – at least this gets you a little readership in exchange for your "surfing for ideas" time. A good traffic exchange offers ratings, and the better blogs get viewed more often. That helps you if you have produced a quality site.

The best part of a traffic exchange is that you will find some sites that are worth linking to, and some good sites will want to share links with you. That little bonus makes it worth a little time surfing around. If nothing else, you will see which blogs are doing well and which ones have no chance. This should help you design a better blog.

After you have tried and tired of this, you might purchase some of the surplus visitors your exchange offers. These visitors might not produce a whole lot for you, but some may want to link to your site – and that's always good.

Banner advertising on these exchanges is also cheap and will target your visitors, unlike the straight purchase of surplus visitors. Again, any hits to your site can generate interest and links.

Exchanges usually require a banner to run on your site also. It's a fair exchange, and a couple of these won't hurt you, regardless of what you think. Remember, you are just getting started. Surf around, join a few, give'em a try. You'll live.

For years now, Yahoo! has been asking viewers to "suggest a site," which allows them to add your site to their search engine. Blogs are popular enough now that there are blog directories that do much the same thing. You visit directories like Bloghub.com, Blogcategory.com, and Blogwise.com and submit your site. Make sure you are very accurate with your description. You will do much better if visitors know what they are getting before they arrive at your blog. Don't misrepresent yourself; it will only waste a lot of people's time and possibly get you kicked off the directory.

Directories usually require a banner ad be placed on your site, just as the traffic exchanges do. Don't worry; there will still be room for your actual logs.

Joining similar blogs in a blog ring can be beneficial for everyone involved. Surf around for a blog ring that features the same content that you do, and check out their features. Usually, you will be able to join immediately, and while visitors will leave your site to check out other similar blogs, you will get visitors from other blogs, and since you will have the best blog, you will get the most repeat visitors. Remember it's all right to play in traffic on the web!

A very similar idea to this is an exchange of links with other blogs that is coordinated through a link exchange. When your page shows the links of other blogs you get credits (based on your traffic or page views), and those credits are returned in the exchange for impressions of your blog on other blog sites.

Try to find an exchange that supports a subject matter grouping, so your impressions are not being met by flashing your blog name on sites who's visitors aren't interested in your particular blog. What good is a link on a baseball site if you write a blog about fashion? And, you need to be aware that the links you are offering may be offensive to some of your readers.

Speed is also an issue if the banners being loaded are Java applications, which will slow down the time it takes to load your page. Surfers hate to wait. Check your site often, and if you find this to be a problem, opt back out of the exchange. It's not worth it.

Another consideration is how the links will appear on your site. You don't want your soothing background and beautiful graphics ruined by a huge yellow monkey swinging from a vine. If you can't modify the application to make it fit your blog, dump it. Again, it's not worth it.

Surf around using your search function and make sure you look at some popular exchanges like *Link2blogs.com*, *LinksPal.com* and *Gotlinks.com*. You might eventually need to consider the use of a service like *LinkExchang com*, which manages your link exchange requests.

If you are industrious, you can also set up your own link exchange at *Linkmarket.com*. Go check 'em out!

Unlike a situation where you are selling books online, and your competition is Amazon, other blogs don't necessarily need to be the enemy. Sure, some are scary because they are professionally maintained and drive tons of traffic, but every single one of them can be an adversary.

Blogs usually allow comments (Do it!) because readers love to see their name, email, or blog mentioned in print, even if they are the ones who mentioned it. This allows you to get free publicity for your own site. Make quality comments in somebody else's blog and leave your calling card. That little advertisement may be on the web forever – try to beat that for a great opportunity!

In fact, the best part of blogs *is* the comment section. Readers leave their comments, and they continue to follow the line of comments to a particular log for days, sometimes even weeks. Your comment and blog address can be seen over and over again. If you made quality comments, readers may drop by your blog to see if you are just a fill-in chef or can really cook.

Don't get yourself banned from another blog by spamming with worthless comments. That's no way to earn a good reputation, and it won't earn you a link from the host. If you do get a link, make sure you return the favor. Write quality blogs, write quality comments, and you will get quality links – probably from sites with a lot more traffic that your site offers. Ain't it a great world?

And now, the bad news: you only have so many links you can offer. Even though your links may not be as good as gold while you build a quality site with high traffic, someday they will be worth a lot. If you give them all away at bargain prices now, you won't have anything to offer in the future. Geez, always a catch!

You will want to check the popularity of your blog. You can do an Internet search for pages that link to you at SEOLogic.com Just follow the directions (type in your web address), and you will be shown the pages that list your URL.

If they are blogs, you might want to take a look at them and see if they warrant an exchange link or a few comments in one of their logs. But again, make sure you consider your links to be valuable. Make sure each one you offer points to a blog that is also bringing visitors to your site. If they don't, pull the plug on 'em, it's the right thing to do.

Search engines are important to your success, but there are only three that are worth anything these days: Google, Yahoo!, and MSN. The remaining 2500 or so don't account for 5% of all the web searches – so why bother with them. If you get an offer to have your site submitted to all those other sites, even for free, what the business making the offer really wants is your email address.

Your new blog host probably offers free blog pinging anyway. You choose which sites to submit your blog to, and an automatic submission engine pings the sites each time you update your blog.

Chapter Nine

Playing the Field

Monogamy is too cruel a rule for bloggers. Sure, you want to be true to your readers, but what if there are readers out there who haven't had a chance to read your work? Don't save yourself for your blog. Blog for others when the price is right.

That price is usually nothing more than a front-page listing of your comments or blog on another blog, but that's what it's all about. There is no such thing as bad publicity, and you need every bit you can get. As you get more popular, other blogs will want you to offer a little insight, even if the subject matter isn't exactly what you usually blog about. A sportswriter who usually follows hockey can still write about the challenges of sports, sports medicine, contracts, agents – you get the drift.

And oh, how those reciprocal links with heavy-traffic sites will help your traffic! Consider your blogging on other sites to be a tradeoff to entice new visitors to your blog. You give the first sample for free, they pay (at least with traffic) for additional words of wisdom available only at your site.

When you first get started, you should search the web for blogs that offer similar content as your own, and convince the owners that they need you to blog for them. Provide quality work for them, and the site owners will be happy, the readers will be happy, and your own advertisers will be happy to pay you higher fees to advertise on your now more popular site.

If you have jokes to offer, trade them for links. Got creative pictures: cats hanging from trees, dogs chasing balls? You name it; you can get a link out of it. Trade your work for links and boost your traffic.

Can you cartoon? Oh, but if you could, don't you think you could do some great trades? Now, keep your brain working here and think of what you do have to offer. Sure, you've got your usual words of wisdom, but do you have more? The possibilities are endless and your talents limitless. Turn your ideas into links!

If you want to push your visitor count up a little, you can buy some "guaranteed" web traffic, but most of this is provided via a pop-up of your web page in a small browser. This is annoying for a surfer and usually, results in an immediate delete of your site. It won't garner you more true visitors, just page hits.

If you do consider buying some web traffic, make sure it is targeted to where you are. If you live in the US or Canada, it doesn't do you much good to have the latest 10,000 hits come from China, now does it?

Now that you have some rudimentary understanding of blogging, and you have a host, a site, and a strong desire to write, get to it. You need to write your blog every day, even more than daily if you have the ability and the time. Readers return for new items on a regular basis. Don't disappoint them.

You may not have the time to write all day long, but use your time wisely and craft some quality work. Blog and respond to comments. If you need help with "comments," consider a service such as *Haloscan.com*, which offers free comments, ratings, and trackback.

Of course you will be trading some ad space for these free services, but the "comments" section of most blogs is what drives much of the traffic. Nothing you blog about will be universally accepted. There will be comments – and that's great. Readers will return to see what their comments generated in response, and may respond again. That's the fun of blogs.

Keep in mind that there are some monitoring and moderation that needs to be done with all "comment" and "feedback" sections. You can't let arguments get too far out of line, or too far off track. If you don't have time to work as a moderator, *Haloscan* can help, as can many other software providers.

While the "comments" section may be a wonderful thing, you will need to keep an eye on it, even if you are using an outside moderator. Occasionally you will have to suspend a reader's ability to comment, or you may need to ban certain people. This may be because they are ignoring the rules of common decency because they are spamming for their own agenda, or for other reasons.

Publish sensible rules for commenting on your blog, and you will reduce the need to ban readers from your comments section. Don't feel bad if you have to ban somebody. It happens. And usually, it's for good. A spamming feind or crazy "comments" guy will drive away your readers – and that's not what it's all about.

Chapter Ten

XML and RSS Feeds

As a successful blogger, you want to make sure your readers have a chance to obtain your blogs each and every day. To make sure your readers have a chance to see your headlines, you can use an RSS feed that the customer clicks on to use on their web browser. This allows them to see what you have without actually going to your site.

RSS is an acronym for Really Simple Syndication or Rich Site Summary. This new technology has produced a very cost-effective method to take your information directly to your clients. RSS allows your blog (or any website) to continually bring Internet surfers the latest news and information from *your* blog. Essentially, RSS is nothing more than a file that shows your information. But if your blog is fun and exciting, readers can and will simply click on a link that will show up on their toolbar to capture your information, any time they wish.

RSS augments the visibility of your website, and increases traffic. The best feature of RSS is that it is lightweight, requiring less than a hundred kilobytes of space. As an XML document, it can be written using any text editor. It remains topical by highlighting what you deem to be most important to your readers.

RSS allows your viewers to enjoy your website because it works well in all browsers – it works on all platforms. If you have done your homework while producing your website and blog, you know what your audience wants. You have taken steps to attract an audience that will continue to be interested in your writing, and they can have a dose every day, just by clicking a single button. You, on the other hand, will collect valuable information about your viewer's habits: number of subscribers, the topics they are interested in, how often they come to your site, and how long they stay.

Each of these items helps you gear your next blog entry towards relevant information, and towards what your viewers are interested in. Take the time to view this information on a regular basis.

If readers are spending all their time on specific topics, or specific pages of your website, that's what you want to concentrate on – while also figuring out where you went wrong on the pages that get very few hits. As you continue to pull in more viewers and more "regulars," your search engine rankings will improve.

When you create an RSS document, you place your current information with an embedded text about the file, such as the current topic, author, etc. This metadata and RSS document is then submitted to an RSS publisher to be registered. After this, anybody using an RSS reader can get it your information from the publisher or directly from your site or blog.

Your RSS document contains a title, a description of the latest item, and a link to the file. Your files are grouped into a channel - the name you assign to your ongoing series of RSS documents. These documents are created in Extensible Markup Language or XML. The HTML tags tell your Internet browser how to display your content while the XML tags define the nature of the available information.

The XML file can be updated manually or by using modules to increase the speed of the process. The feed is prepared by transforming the RSS file into HTML. Once changed by server-side, your files are placed in a template and made available to readers from your website or by registering your feed to content aggregators, or other websites that list various feeds. The entire process sounds intimidating, but by skating around Google a bit, you can find all the information you need!

Individual RSS readers can subscribe to your blog, and other websites can do the same. Reciprocal trades with other sites will provide your site visitors with new information. You can't be everything to everyone and will need to have additional information for your visitors, or they will soon tire of the same old content. Choose your reciprocal links carefully, and you can increase your traffic flow considerably while keeping your current readers happy.

If you want more information on the technology behind RSS/XML, a good place to start is *XML.com*. An RSS feed allows you to syndicate your content, much like a syndicated columnist provides content to a group of newspapers, which allows other bloggers to provide real-time links to your information. Moving your content out of your blog and onto the blogs of others is one of the greatest features of whatever blog software you use.

Surfers who want RSS feeds need only download and install a free RSS newsreader client. Many are available (some as browser extensions). Then, they simply point their software to RSS feeds of interest, and they are done!

For the publisher (you), syndicates such as *Syndic8.com, Feedster.com,* or *NewsisFree.com* are good places to start your search.

Networked Blogs is a Facebook App that allows you to create your own type of syndication. It's a very good start for new bloggers.

Chapter Eleven

Putting it All Together

Your Blog business, to be profitable, must generate sufficient income to cover not only your actual costs but to pay you for your time and expertise. The costs you can keep under control by intelligently managing the money you spend on promotion and marketing. You manage potential customers by attracting and keeping readers interested. But to make a profit, you've got to make sales. We've talked about clicks, links, and swag. Let's go deeper.

Growing an Offline Business

You may have a physical business you want to grow by writing a blog. Sell Pizzas? You should be blogging about your location, your menu, special events, your hours, your great employees (won't they send family and friends to your blog?) and so many more things. Let your mind wander!

Selling Products

Online Products that you can add links to (in very catchy and informative places in your blogs) include eBooks, software, reports, Apps, audio webinars, and of course those catchy YouTube videos you're making to promote your blog.

What, no videos? You can make your own using software such as *Power Point* – get to work!

Physical Products

Any products can be sold via your blog or ads on your pages, but books and DVD's are very popular. If you join Amazon, make widgets for books you blog about and collect that commission!

Don't know how affiliate sales work with Amazon? Look! Content items such as premium content, coaching, and training are also possibilities.

Services

Again, coaching and training services can be offered by you or your advertisers. Who wants to learn how to make the best pizza possible at home? Can you teach someone to do that? Sell them an eBook about it, or a video – that can only be accessed after they pay for it on Paypal.

How about a monthly subscription service? That's another thing Paypal can do for you - collecting a subscription fee. How about consulting? Can you offer freelance writing?

Advertising

There are a lot of possibilities for income production here: Ad networks, sponsorships, text links, pay per posts, CPC (Cost per click programs), CPM (Cost per impression programs), newsletters you email to your subscribers that carry ads, and there's still more!

Selling clicks is a method used by most websites these days. When you place a link, whether a simple text link or a banner advertisement, you hope some of your readers will click them and make you money. Some ads bring you income based on how many web impressions the ad gets (which is the same as saying you get paid each time a visitor opens your web page).

With clicks, you are selling other advertisers a chance to capture some of your customers. If you place a link to Amazon, and a customer clicks the link and buys a book, you get paid a percentage of the purchase as an *associate*.

Your readers won't like all of the ads on your blog, but surfers are used to a certain amount of advertising being displayed on their favorite sites. Just make sure you don't drown them in ads. As for the ads themselves, make sure you are accepting only advertising that at least isn't offensive to your readers.

If you publish a blog about baseball, your readers won't mind ads for team caps. They probably won't mind something from Amazon or Google, but they start wondering what's going on when there are ads for a septic system product. Think ahead to what should work, and what might not work.

Unfortunately, most advertising these days is done with Java applets. These ads load slowly and bog down your blog. You may need one or two of these, but don't get so greedy that your readers leave due to slow page changes. And, stay away from popups.

Nobody likes popups. They open additional browsers and are a general pain in the blog. They too slow down your page loads and should be avoided if at all possible.

Creating your advertising income program should be simple (at least from this one aspect), don't allow the kind of ads that you hate! Flashing ads and ads that float across the page are the least liked of all. Dump 'em.

Another ad campaign that has become so commonplace that most surfers don't mind them are the fairly unobtrusive ads placed by Yahoo!, Google, and MSN that feature products similar to what your web page offers.

Again, if you blog about baseball, Google's AdSense will feature ads that are from ticket sellers, memorabilia sellers, etc. It's usually a reasonable match and doesn't seem too obtrusive, but weight what you make from them against what you could make with widgets from Amazon for the same products!

When one of your readers clicks on an AdSense advertising link, you get paid a portion of what the advertiser is paying Google for the "hit." The payment can be quite reasonable, and there are many popular blogs that make a good income just from Adsense.

Before signing up with Google, do a web search for some of the other adword programs and check some blogs and see what looks good to you. Then, compare payment programs, income levels, and then go through the process of signing up with your chosen one.

Associate selling, as with Amazon, can also boost your income. With some these sites, any item that sells from a click on your website link will put money in your bank account, usually 4 to 7 percent of the purchase price. That's the best part.

The downside is that you only get paid on the first purchase. The "cookie" from your link may stay active for 30-days or more (and you will get credit from purchases for up to that 30-days), but only for the first purchase.

If you like the idea of making money as an associate, you might consider going to *CommissionJunction.com* to check out the program they have. You sign up with *CJ*, and then pick associate deals from hundreds being offered. *CJ* does all the legwork, collects your fees, and pays you in one lump sum each month. So easy!

There are also some multi-level programs that pay you a fee, then pay you an additional fee from the income produced by any associates who join through your link. This can provide a long line of income

You can also sell advertising space based on time, or impressions (those page views again). In this case, you place the link or banner advertising for your buyer and let the ad run until your site has generated xxx number of visitors, or their month is us – depending on what you agreed to provide. You can solicit this business yourself by finding websites that feature similar products to those you blog about. Don't be shy. You might start at $5 a month for a small ad.

Go ahead and make a name for yourself as a reliable blogger, an expert in your field, and a high traffic location, and then focus on selling those banner impressions. While you may need to do some convincing, you *can* do it.

When you do manage to sell a few advertisers on your blog, don't become a shill for their products. Readers don't want to read your baseball blog and hear why Big Bob's Ticket Exchange is the best ticket company in the world each week while looking at Big Bob's banner ad right next to your blog. Sure, you can mention your advertisers, but don't go overboard.

As for the sale of "swag," or products that feature your blog name (shirts, coffee mugs, mouse pads, etc.), wait until you have a reasonable number of steady readers before you buys these advertising products in bulk. Specialty advertising items like key chain's, golf tees, etc. are fun to give away and sell, but small orders are very expensive due to the custom printing.

When you purchase these items in sufficient quantities, the price is very reasonable, and you can make a few dollars with each sale. That's not the only reason you want to sell them, but the time involved in packaging the items and sending them off must be counted. Your time is valuable.

If you have just a few items, most websites allow you to offer Paypal links to handle the purchase. Or, you can use an eBay store. If you prefer, you can even run your products as a continuing eBay sale using the "Buy it now" option. Then, you link the photo of your product on your blog site to your eBay sale. If the customer has an eBay account (doesn't everybody?), they can make the purchase.

On the other hand, if the customer has an Amazon account, you might entice them to make a donation to you simply because when they arrived at your blog site, they saw their name pop up on an Amazon Honor System banner.

With the donation system Amazon has set up, the readers don't need an Amazon account, and you can get some free cash to keep your site afloat. Join Amazon and get a tiny piece of HTML code to add to your blog. The code displays a banner or button that allows your readers to make a donation of from $1 to $50. What a deal (well, Amazon does take a small cut)!

Paypal also offers donations- by-credit-card program. Also, you and your readers can setup a monthly subscription to your blog, to special reports, to email-only programs, etc.

Most website software allows special secure areas that require a password to enter. You can archive your special reports in one area, and allow entry only by a purchased password. You make the password good only for the length of the subscription, and you are getting a monthly fee for your writing!

As you continue to blog, you will eventually have quite a collection of archived information. If you are also producing special reports, then new subscribers will like the fact that they get not only the current issues, but all the back issues. The longer you have been offering the service, the better deal new subscribers will get.

If you start out sending these reports via email, you still might want to move forward at some point to the secure website just to offer those back issues. Your readers will look forward to new reports, but they will eventually want to find past reports in one place.

Another thing your readers will want is your continued submission of quality blogs and reports. You can't sell a one-year, monthly subscription and then only send out an issue every six weeks or when you get around to it. Your readers are loyal to you – return that loyalty by fulfilling your end of the bargain.

EBooks are fairly popular right now. The information they provide can be valuable, although by the time many readers get the books the information is often dated. However, most eBooks are filled through an auto responder.

Email auto responders are a feature of most website email programs. When a customer sends an email to your site, your auto responder sends a response that you have already written. You may set up some different responses, for each of your email accounts. A Q&A email might respond: "Thank you for your question, we will be in touch shortly," or something similar.

You can sell your eBooks, or subscriptions in the same manner. An autoresponder can send your new customer the password or code necessary to access the purchased archive or eBook. You can be sound asleep or surfing in Oahu while your customers are buying, and receive your product.

Companies like *Aweber.com* and *iContact.com* sell "packaged" auto responder programs. Surf around, see what you like – and take advantage of one of the easier, and most profitable aspects of your blog site.

These ideas are only a start. There are plenty of other ways to improve your viewership, improve your income, and improve your writing. Of these three, the one we didn't touch on much was writing.

If you have a love of writing, you probably have a rudimentary understanding of how to form words into sentences, sentences into paragraphs, and paragraphs into a story, column, or simple blog. If you have trouble with grammar and punctuation, I suggest you spend the six or seven bucks it will cost to get a copy of *The Elements of Style*, by William Strunk. It's a small book, under a hundred pages, and is invaluable. If you need help with the writing itself, surf around and find some websites that writers visit.

I enjoy the Science Fiction and Fantasy Writers of America site at *SFWA.org*. I'm not a big fan of Science Fiction, but the advice found at the website is excellent. You also might take a look at *WritersPublishingGroup.com*, which features pages of advice for writers – especially those who are trying to get published.

Another excellent resource is Book Blogs, which is really about what it says: blogs on books, but you can wander around (virtually) and see how the site is designed to help bloggers network.

Certainly, Facebook and Twitter are options, but everything comes back to writing a good blog. The marketing aspects of getting your name and your blog out there where people can enjoy it are a big step. Once you have several posts on your blog, that's the time to search the internet for blogs similar to your own and start leaving comments, asking the bloggers themselves for link exchanges, and then doing the Facebook and Twitter thing to try and drive more interest.

Sensory Overload

At this point, you probably have quite a bit of sensory overload from what you've learned. Let's recap a tiny bit for the cash impaired: find a niche you love, use a popular free blog site, start your blog with a catchy name that others will search for, post pictures and words about that niche name, start networking, and do some other articles for other sites.

Why the other articles? Because other sites already have a fan base, and you don't. Every article you write elsewhere can bring readers to your blog – and it's free. All you are investing in those articles (besides your hard work) is your time.

Yahoo Contributors Network can give you a chance to sell some articles and get some readers. It's not my favorite, but you can get some name recognition if you write well on popular subjects.

You might want to consider *Hubpages.com*, also. You get paid based on page views, and it will help you learn how to format and do articles (just like your blog) on a regular basis. The more articles you do, the more you can make.

No, that's not what this book is about (remember, blogging), but it will give you a chance to link to your own blog (and search engines love organic links). The more popular the website you link from, but more Google likes it, so a link from Joe's blog with five subscribers barely gets noticed, but a link from a site with wide readership does get noticed.

If you want to become an expert to enhance your blogging, consider joining a group like *Examiner.com*. You'll need to prove you can write, and find an opening in your local that needs an examiner, but the recognition can be very helpful, and an occasional link to an excellent article elsewhere is tolerated. And, you do get paid for page views, so this is a paying gig. Filling out an application is easy, and once you have written some articles, you can make money by referring new writers.

Regardless of where you start, you have to start.

Now that you have built up a few rows of bricks, it will soon be time to write your first blog. This should be a memorable moment, so spend plenty of time mulling over what you want to say before starting. Then, get the words down on your word processor. You might want to wait for 24-hours before looking at what you have written, and then after a second, or even a third look (plus grammar and spell checker) paste that puppy into your blog.

Don't be shy – it's time. Now, consider what's next on your blog plate. What's the next entry going to be? Pace yourself and remember that you always want your content to be fresh and interesting.

A Little About Search Engines

Search engines like Google have algorithms that take into account many things about web pages before boosting their ranking and associated listing on search pages. You can't beat the new software; you can only adapt and provide good blogs.

You can't "buy" hits and improve your ranking because the software tracks how long each subject is on your page. If they go to your page for 2 seconds and click away, that hurts you. If they go to your page and stay awhile, click on more posts or pages, then it's a "quality" search. If they do not go back and search the same product you are golden.

Your blog also needs backlinks from other websites. The better those sites, the better you score with the search engines. A bunch of links from web pages nobody ever reads is junk. Don't waste any effort or money on getting them. Get quality links from real sites and your site will be considered high quality.

Chapter Twelve

The Final Key to Success

Being a successful blogger isn't hard, but you have to be able to write. You need to be consistent, innovative, and you have to work well with others. You also want to choose a blog name that may show up on search engine pages from a keyword search. If you call your blog *Banana Boat* and blog about horses, that's going to be a problem.

Search engines are attracted to keywords, then page views and continuing addition of quality content, and then links (in and out). Use relevant keywords in your blog name, your blogs, and your article pages!

The better your product, the higher you are listed in a search. If you are never on Goggle's front page, how are you going to be seen? To understand this, do a quick search – Google: *Nevada casino history*. Yup, that's my blog – listed first!

Don't view more successful bloggers as competition; view them as a vast expanse of colleagues with a wealth of knowledge you should emulate. Follow their leads and don't be afraid to ask for help, create blogrolls and link to their sites.

Mentioning excellent sites in your blogs can bring you reciprocal links that greatly enhance your stature! And, some of those great sites may link back to your blog.

You need those backlinks for good SEO (Search engine optimization) to rate well with search engines like Yahoo! and Google. They are very important. Also important are all the links from your blog to your other writing. If you are taking advantage of places like Hubpages.com wher you are paid by page views, don't you want new readers to find those pages?

The Final Key

So now you've got the idea of how blogging works. Perhaps you have even started a blog, created links, written articles to get your name out, used blog comments to get backlinks, contacted other blogs, offered advertising or signed up with Adwords, found a few perfect items to sell through an affiliate, got something going with Amazon, and started Tweeting about your amazing blog and still something is missing. What could it be?

The final key is giving your readers a reason to come back to your blog! If you can hook them into subscribing to an automatic email feed when you post or an RSS feed – well that's great, but will they read it or click to see what else you are offering?

Ah, the real secret of successful blogging – great content. That's right; you have to give your readers a reason to come back. I'm not just talking about ending a blog with "next week we have freebies to give away," or something in that vein.

If you have a blog about *cats* and every blog is about *Persian cats*, well, you just cut your traffic by 95%. Is that what you want? If it is, you should have called your blog Persian Cats instead of Cats. Bummer!

However, if that's the direction you are going, make sure every blog has something new: photos, little-known facts, links to articles and books about your new subject, and a little humor never hurts.

And what can you make? That's the big question, right? It all depends on your ability to write entertaining blogs, get links in place to other blogs, and get some traffic. If you help support yourself by getting people to click on links to your articles on other sites, that's a great way to start making money.

If you have your book, you should be able to convert about .5 percent to 1 percent of all visitors who came to your site looking for a book or product about your subject. That's a book sale for every 100 to 200 visitors. Now you know why I blog about my favorite subject, old casinos – because I write books about old casinos – and I sell a lot of books.

Spend a few minutes right now thinking about what you would want to find each time you went to a blog – or subscribed. That's your key to success – repeat business.

Once you have the hook to get them back (maybe your amazing writing is really enough – you will find out quickly), put it into place on your blog. I hope it is something you can be proud of, and that now you are well on your way to fulfilling your dream of writing a blog and making a profit doing so.

Let Me Hold Your Hand

In case you are still frightened about starting your own blog, I have additional help and free marketing if you click on my Author Book Marketing blog that I started just to show you how easy the process is (www.authorbookmarketing.blogspot.com). As long as your blog is reasonably put together (no adult or mean things), I'll list you for free backlinks, get you some startup traffic, and we'll both see how you do. You are welcome to ask questions as you go. The truth is, you're going to need a little marketing.

I chose a title (Author Book Marketing) that I have a clear interest in, and I checked with blogger.com to see if it was available. How easy is that? Just go to the upper right corner and click on *create a blog*. That link will take you to blogger's home page and let you create an account. There is no fee. I am not an affiliate.

From your overview screen, you can set up your entire blog in just a few minutes by clicking on the appropriate links on the left side of the screen. Here are the easy steps.

Choose a *template* (the background that you see) from a long list of designs (you can change any time you want without losing your info) and then chose a layout.

The *layout* sets the size of each blog post and where any extras like your personal profile and photo go. Click on *posts* to enter a new blog post. Click on *settings* to put a description of your blog at the top of the front page.

Click on *earnings* to sign up for Google Affiliate ads.

Click on *pages* to post individual pages that your readers can access by clicking on a tab – these are not blogs, but individual pages for expanded subjects or places to emphasize items you are selling!

Now go back to the *layout* link and click on one of the *add a gadget* links. Scroll down the list of items you can add and check them out. Which ones do you want on your blog?

Add a few simple ones like *favorite posts* or the *Google+* gadget to see how they look on your new blog. Now you are cooking! And, now you are momentarily on your own.

Keep experimenting. Keep checking other blogs to get new ideas. Click on the page tabs on *Author Book Marketing* to get even more ideas and advice! My goal with most of my blogs is to sell my books, not to maximize sales for other people.

Your goal for your blog may be quite different. If you have no products of your own, your goal may be to write at your leisure and make income from affiliate sales, or from advertising, or from any of the other forms of marketing you can provide – or all of them. That's your little red wagon, as they say.

Regardless, start by simply writing a fun, engaging blog with great posts and photos that readers will return to see more of. That's the best goal you can reach quickly. Write, learn, expand, experiment, and succeed!

Once you have a few posts, contact everyone on your email list of friends and relatives. Send them a nice email and let them know about your great new blog. Ask them to take a look, using the link you provide in the email. Then start reading about marketing your blog!

In the future, I hope you can blog successfully from your own boat, sailing the warm Pacific, or from a cold and windy tent high in the Himalayan Mountains, if that's your bent. There is no reason you can't achieve these things – just log on, and blog on.

And, you know about Twitter, and Facebook, and Pinterest, and…well, you'll want to signup for each, link them to your blog, and keep that publicity going. People want entertainment. You can provide it!